Virtual Reality in Religion and Spirituality

Exploring Faith in the Digital Age

Table of Contents

The future of communication is certainly going to be through virtual reality.

— Ram Shriram

Chapter 1. Introduction

In the intricate intersection of technology and spirituality, a profound transformation is taking place, shaping our understanding and practice of faith in awe-inspiring ways. Our special report delves into the fascinating realm of "Virtual Reality in Religion and Spirituality: Exploring Faith in the Digital Age." The narrative of this illuminating report is woven with vibrant threads of captivating case studies, insightful expert perspectives, and profound observations. We will take you on an extraordinary journey where timeless traditions meet cutting-edge technology, revealing how virtual reality is revolutionizing religious experiences and practices, making them more accessible, immersive, and personalized. This expertly crafted report is bound to pique your curiosity and broaden your horizons. Immerse yourself into this enthralling exploration and discover the transforming landscape of faith in the 21st Century. Your adventure in this innovative spiritual frontier begins here, ensuring you'd want to secure this riveting must-read special report!

Chapter 2. Understanding Virtual Reality: An Introduction

Virtual reality (VR) is a technological phenomenon sweeping across a vast landscape of industries - offering unprecedented opportunities for users to transcend the constraints of physical reality and explore a fully immersive, artificial world. This introductory chapter aims to provide a comprehensive understanding of this transformative technology, beginning with its definition and fundamental principles, offering an examination of its technical components, and concluding with its potential implications for various sectors, with a particular emphasis on its intriguing intersection with religion and spirituality.

2.1. Understanding the Concept of Virtual Reality

Virtual reality is best described as a simulated environment created by computer technology, creating a world that users can interact with by means of a VR headset or similar device. These environments are typically constructed in 3D and can mimic the physical world or take on fantastic, imaginative landscapes. The primary objective of VR is to create a convincing, immersive illusion of reality which allows the user to feel as if they are in another place.

In the context of VR, "immersion" is a term frequently used to describe the sensation of being in a completely different environment. Immersion can be gauged in two ways: physically and psychologically. Physical immersion is experienced when users feel as if they are truly present in the virtual environment, often achieved through combination of visual, auditory, and sometimes tactile feedback. Psychological immersion, on the other hand, refers to the emotional engagement or depth of involvement that users feel within the VR experience.

2.2. Components of Virtual Reality Systems

Critical to understanding virtual reality is a grasp of the three essential technological components of VR systems: the computer/software, the display, and the tracking system.

The Computer/Software: The computer and software serve as the 'brain' of the virtual reality system, generating the interactive 3D environment, and rendering the high-definition graphics necessary for a satisfactory user experience. To create complex virtual environments that are convincing, the software often incorporates real-world physics to simulate gravity, light, wind, and other natural elements.

The Display: While there are numerous types of VR displays available on the market, the most commonly utilized in consumer products are Head-Mounted Displays (HMDs). These devices, worn like a helmet or a pair of goggles, create the illusion of immersion by covering the user's field of vision with digital imagery. Modern VR headsets are equipped with stereoscopic displays, directing slightly different images to each eye, thereby simulating depth and enhancing the realism of the virtual environment.

The Tracking System: This component is responsible for constantly monitoring the user's position and movements and translating them into the virtual world. There are various tracking systems within a VR setup, including those that track head movement, hand movement, and, in some cases, full-body movement.

2.3. Virtual Reality: A Revolutionary Tool

The potential applications of virtual reality are far-reaching and transformative. VR is not only revolutionizing gaming and entertainment but also infiltrating sectors such as education, medicine, architecture, military training, and, intriguingly, the domain of religion and spirituality. The following chapters aim to illustrate the fascinating ways in which VR is changing how we understand, experience, and practice religion.

As the curtain lifts on this exciting story of the intersection of faith and technology, it is imperative to understand VR's potential not only as a tool of modern entertainment, but as a catalyst of profound change. With its ability to immerse users in a simulated world, virtual reality offers an unparalleled platform for spiritual exploration, facilitating strikingly vivid religious experiences otherwise unattainable in the physical world. This book guides readers through the fascinating narrative of this emerging trend, underscored by enlightening case studies and expert commentaries, offering a captivating journey through the transformative impact of VR on the realm of faith and spirituality.

So, as we ascend into the digital realm, let's ready ourselves for a deep dive into understanding not just WHAT virtual reality is, but also HOW it is poised to reframe our spiritual experiences and interactions. Stay tuned for the captivating interplay of tradition and technology, set to reshape the contours of faith in the 21st Century in ways previously unimagined.

Chapter 3. History of Virtual Reality in Religion: A Retrospective Glimpse

Virtual Reality (VR), once confined to the realm of computer-aided design and video games, has found strong alignments with the practice of religion and spirituality. The resilient roots of this association trace back to the initial thrust of technological advancements, creating a rich tapestry of a history interspersed with significant milestones.

3.1. Early Years: Primitive Technological Immersion

The inception of VR's journey in the domain of the sacred was grounded in the eagerness to recreate religious sanctity and bring its meaning closer to practitioners far and wide. Although not recognized as 'VR' then, the essence of this technology was born in the pioneered attempts of virtual simulation and immersion.

The panoramas of the nineteenth century, showcasing landscapes or historical scenes, was possibly an early inception of VR. These subtleties characterizing 360-degree view paintings were designed to immerse the observer into a different world, venturing to trigger a similar effect as modern VR does today. Integrating the spiritual narratives in these settings broadened the immersive experience, creating rudimentary enactments of important religious contexts.

Progressing forward, the Stereoscope, introduced by Sir Charles Wheatstone in 1838, provided 3D images and visuals. This advancement gave birth to a novel way to perceive religious images, narratives, and symbols. It marked the precursor to the evolution of technology aiming to transport individuals to altered states of reality, drawing them closer to their faith and belief systems.

3.2. Advent of Virtual Reality: The 20th Century

The 20th century began with an increasing focus on dedicated VR technology. Morton Heilig, often acknowledged as the 'Father of Virtual Reality,' patented the Sensorama machine in the 1960s. Although not used for religious practices, this technology demonstrated the power of VR as an all-encompassing sensory experience.

The conceptual groundwork laid by Sensorama was picked up by Ivan Sutherland who built the first head-mounted display system for immersive simulation, stretched towards educational and military purposes initially. The eventual translation of these revolutionary inventions to religious and spiritual atmospheres was a promising certainty.

One notable intersection of VR and spirituality during this period was the creation of the cybersect – a religious group or faith that primarily functions in the virtual world. This concept, although not widely accepted by the traditional church bodies, nevertheless offered a new perspective on religious expression and practice through the lens of evolving technology.

3.3. Infancy of Virtual Reality in Religion: Late 20th Century

As we stepped into the digital age, the adoption of VR technology in religious practices gained genuine momentum. From the late 90s until the early 2000s, several immersive VR applications emerged, providing a platform for believers to engage with faith in exciting, unconventional ways.

An early instance was the VR installation named "PLACE-Hampi," which offered a virtual tour of the Vijayangar temple in Hampi, a UNESCO World Heritage site. This immersive VR experience aimed to evoke a heightened sense of religious engagement by transporting users to an environment brimming with spiritual significance. The success of such applications underscored the transformative potential of VR in religious contexts, leading the way for future endeavors.

The emergence of Second Life, an internet-based virtual world launched in 2003, was a game-changer. It allowed for the creation and exploration of various religious spaces and experiences, taking the concepts of worship, prayer, learning, and community into an unprecedented digital realm. This unique approach offered a taste of the immense potential that lies at the intersection of VR and religion.

3.4. Milestones and Advances of the 21st Century

At the break of the 21st century, emerged innovative and compelling applications of VR in the sphere of religion and spirituality. As technology evolved, so did the efforts to present more sophisticated, interactive, and realistic virtual experiences that could cater to the growing demand for such spiritual offerings.

From the VR installation at London's historic St John's Church to the Church of Sweden's Minecraft server initiative "KyrkCraft," several explorations opened new opportunities for believers to connect with their faith practices in unimaginable ways. Numerous apps and platforms, such as VRChat and AltVR, were brought into play to construct religiously significant spaces, services, and fellowship.

The advancement also reached contemplation and meditation

practices, where VR luxury suites or apps like 'VR Retreat' offered users an escape from their daily routine to ascend into a soothing, meaningful, virtual experience.

In conclusion, the journey of VR's incorporation into religious practices is an absorbing tale of technological paradigm shifts transforming spirituality. From early panoramas to cutting-edge VR applications, the progress has been remarkable. Certainly, this is just the beginning, and the future seems brimming with even more exceptional advancements that will continue to redefine faith with the 'real' in virtual reality. This revolution stands as a testament to the human desire for spiritual exploration and the unceasing innovation that caters to this yearning, deepening our understanding of VR's role in the domain of religion and its continued evolution.

Chapter 4. The Modern Shift: Binging Religion into the Virtual Realm

In the early days, virtual reality (VR), with all its potential in various aspects of life, was largely seen as a tool of entertainment. It soon invaded academic and scientific fields, later making its way inside military training facilities, the automobile industry, and healthcare. The dawn of the 21st century, however, brought with it an interesting epiphany connecting the sacred with the digital. The concept of virtual reality in religion started gaining momentum, paving the way for a paradigm shift, bouncing atop the wavelength of the digital wave, and surfing into the vast and unfathomable realm of spirituality. This was the modern shift.

4.1. Significance of the Shift

The transformation of religious practice into the digital sphere cannot be minimalized. It denotes not only an evolution in the way we experience faith but also triggers questions about how we perceive reality itself. The virtual world offers unlimited access and freedom to explore spiritual practices without geographical constraints or the need to adhere to time-bound rituals. This shift reinvents the face of modern religious practices, bringing an abstract concept like spirituality into the tangible grasp of technology.

4.2. Dissecting the Shift

Let's dissect this shift in religious virtue and delve deeper into how VR in religion came into play. It started with growing discontent over conventional religious practices and the stringent rules they imposed. Plethora people expressed their need for more flexibility and inclusivity that traditional religious spaces often missed. People wanted to explore faith at their own pace, in their comfort zones, without feeling left out or judgmental eyes. Digital faith was the reaction to this demographic tilt, integrating the world's major religions into the realm of VR, resulting in a more democratic religious environment.

4.3. Rise of Digital Faith

The narrative of digital faith began with a simple yet transformational idea - to create an infinite religious space free from spatial and temporal limits. The first virtual churches and temples sprouted in the online realms of Second Life and similar platforms, where individuals could experience religious events in their avatar form. These were innocuous beginnings, arguably dismissed as novelty or even escapism. However, within these virtual landscapes, interrupted only by the curvature of digital horizons, profound contemplations were being sown.

4.4. Disrupting Traditional Practices

The advent of VR in religious practices was initially met with skepticism and sometimes outright rejection. Religious purists argued that this trend was insulting the sanctity of religion, reducing it to a mere spectacle. They viewed it as an unnecessary intrusion of tech in sacred intervals. However, supporters of VR faith argued that technological advancement and religion are not polar opposites. Instead, they can coexist in harmony and mutually benefit one another. VR in religious practices aims to transcend barriers and make religion a more accessible, personalized experience. It is more about personal spirituality than communal celebration.

4.5. Case in Point: VR Churches

One of the most notable examples that signify the shift is VR Churches. These began with the onset of platforms such as VRChat where congregations in an immersive 3D environment were possible. You can fully immerse yourself in the spiritual experience, navigate through a virtually constructed church, listen to the sermon, sing hymns, and interact with other virtual attendees. This approach has disrupted the conventional understanding and practice of attending church, fostering community, and sharing faith.

4.6. Altering Paths of Pilgrimage

Not just the recurring religious practices, but VR has also altered the paths of pilgrimage. Various organizations have developed VR experiences that take you through virtual tours of pilgrimage sites. The 'Visit in Israel' project is one such example, where one can virtually navigate through religious sites across the country, experiencing their spiritual charm without leaving their homes.

4.7. Intersection of VR and Meditation

Buddhist practices, notably meditation, have also found resonance with VR technologies. Apps like 'Playne' and 'Guided Meditation VR' provide immersive experiences that help users create their meditation spaces, choose serene backdrops, and select guided meditation roles. This intersection between VR tech and meditation hints at how value-driven use of VR can potentially become an essential accessory of progressive spiritual practices.

The modern shift of infusing religion into the virtual realm is still in its infancy, yet its horizon is filled with endless potential. As the digital age advances, the conundrum of the physical vs. the virtual will continue to spark debates. However, one thing is sure - the era of physical restrictions in exploring spirituality is gradually fading, and the dawn of the unrestricted virtual spiritual realm is upon us. The unanimous understanding of faith and spirituality too is getting remodeled, bearing the foundations of unrestrained transcendental exploration. The widespread acceptance of this domain, however, in this technocratic world still remains a question, and rightly so, a matter of personal faith.

Chapter 5. Case Studies: Triumphs of VR in Various Religious Contexts

Investigating the various ways that Virtual Reality (VR) has been used in religious contexts, it becomes clear that there are a number of pioneering case studies that provide evidence of VR's profound impact. These triumphs of VR in the spiritual realm range from immersive religious education to enabling remote participation in rituals and celebrations, to creating virtual communities of worship.

5.1. The Vatican VR: Immersive Education and Pilgrimage from Home

The Vatican, regarded as the spiritual home of the world's 1.2 billion Roman Catholics, has made significant strides in harnessing VR technology to make religious education more engaging and immersive. A fine example of this is "The Vatican VR", an impressive VR project that takes users on a visually rich and engaging journey through the Vatican City. They virtually tour its iconic edifices like St. Peter's Basilica and Sistine Chapel as if they were physically present.

Utilizing high-resolution 3D scans and photorealistic rendering, it provides the faithful with a meticulous representation of these important religious landmarks, imbued with historical and symbolic significance. By offering users a a chance to virtually visit the Vatican and learn about its spiritual, artistic, and cultural heritage, the project caters not only to the physically distant or disabled pilgrims but also to those who seek a more intimate, knowledge-based connection with their faith.

5.2. VR for Hajj: Making the Pilgrimage Accessible

The Hajj, the pilgrimage to Mecca that Muslims are required to make at least once in their lives if physically and financially capable, presents both logistical and practical challenges for the faithful. Yet VR technology has emerged as a powerful tool in addressing these challenges.

A VR experience developed by Labbaik VR offers Muslims a chance to virtually participate in the Hajj rituals from the comfort of their homes. It is especially beneficial for those unable to undertake the journey due to age, health or financial constraints. Besides facilitating spiritual participation, this product also serves as a tool for training and preparing potential pilgrims; visiting Mecca can be overwhelming, so a virtual run-through helps immensely in familiarizing future attendees with the event's rituals.

5.3. Virtual Temples in Hinduism

The virtual revolution has also made its mark in Hinduism. Many sacred Hindu temples in India, which have religious and cultural significance, can be virtually visited through a smartphone or a VR headset. It is a boon for devotees and tourists alike who wish to avoid the physical hardships of traveling or negotiate intense crowd situations.

Moreover, a web-based platform called "SacredVR" is envisaging the creation of 'virtual temples' in virtual space where users can carry out virtual 'pujas' (worship rituals) dedicated to various Hindu deities. Providing both traditionalists and young technologically-savvy devotees a new way of connecting with Hindu spirituality, these virtual temples demonstrate a unique blend of ancient religious traditions and cutting-edge technology.

5.4. Virtual Buddhist Meditation Retreats

Buddhism is another faith embracing the promise of VR. Numerous organizations have developed VR experiences that provide immersive meditation retreats. Within these VR retreats, users can create a customizable and tranquil environment conducive to their own practices - an offering particularly useful amidst the tumult of modern life.

One application, "MindVR", allows users to virtually sit under the Bodhi Tree in India, where Buddha is believed to have achieved enlightenment. This VR experience, in particular, brings the holistic aspects of Buddhism to the digital age, enabling a meditative mind-state, and tranquil reprieve from real-world distractions.

5.5. Conclusion

Careful examination of these case studies makes it apparent how VR technology holds immense potential in enriching religious experiences. Each unique example paints a picture of how different faith traditions have embraced VR as a mechanism to foster spiritual growth, facilitate participation in religious activities, and foster a sense of community. Nevertheless, the realm of VR in religious contexts remains deeply unexplored, offering untold opportunities for further research, implementation, and spiritual innovation.

Chapter 6. Technological Breakthroughs in Virtual Reality: Enriching Faith Experiences

As we delve deeper into the transformative influence of Virtual Reality (VR) on spiritual experiences, it is impossible to overlook the profound role that technological advancements have played in this journey. They have not only remarkably enhanced the technical aspects of virtual practices but also greatly enriched the essence and the quality of faith experiences. From holography to haptic feedback, from photorealistic graphics to advanced auditory systems, each technological leap has served as a unique catalyst in making spiritual practices more immersive, engaging, and personal.

6.1. The Dawn of Photorealistic VR Environments

One of the most enthralling breakthroughs in the VR space that has revolutionized religious experiences is the inception and refinement of photorealistic graphics. This technological innovation has enabled the creation of immersive virtual environments that closely mimic physical religious spaces like temples, churches, synagogues, and mosques, imbuing the virtual realm with a greater semblance of reality. This development has enabled worshippers to virtually transport themselves to these digitally replicated spaces, allowing them to experience a semblance of physical presence while practicing their faith.

The backbone of this immersive experience is the intricate and meticulous use of Polygon mesh, Texturing, Shaders, Lighting, and

Rendering techniques. Each of these elements individually and collectively contributes to meticulously mirroring the architecture, aesthetics, and ambiance of these sacred physical spaces in the virtual realm.

6.2. Haptic Technology: Touching the Virtual

Another major technological milestone in the world of VR is the advent of sophisticated haptic technology. This tactile feedback system enables users to feel and interact with the virtual environment in a more intimate and tangible manner.

Imagine being able to touch a holy symbol, insignia, or artifact in the virtual world and feel its texture, contours, and temperature. Such fine haptic nuances can drastically augment depth and authenticity to digital religious experiences, making them all the more immersive and emotionally resonating.

The driving force behind this technological marvel is a complex interplay of actuators, sensors, and algorithms. The interplay of these elements creates a sophisticated tactile feedback system, which can simulate a wide range of tactile sensations, from the cold touch of a stone altar to the soft feel of a prayer rug beneath the fingertips.

6.3. Hyper-Realistic 3D Audio Systems

In enhancing the quality and depth of virtual religious experiences, the role of auditory systems cannot be overstated. Combining VR visuals with spatial, binaural audio drastically enhances the believability and immersion of the virtual experience.

Advanced auditory systems in VR can recreate echoes, reverberation, and specific acoustic signatures associated with different types of religious structures and spaces. This ability to replicate audio-visual cues associated with specific religious spaces can invoke powerful emotional responses, deeply enriching the virtual faith experience.

6.4. Harnessing the Power of Holography in Virtual Worship

Holography, though a relatively newer entrant in the realm of VR, is rapidly emerging as a game-changer. Holographic technology can project 3D images of religious figures, symbols, and narratives, bringing them to life in the virtual space in a visually astonishing and emotionally moving manner.

The profound impact of such visceral, lifelike representations in the context of faith can't be overstated. By injecting a new level of visual enchantment and emotional depth into digital worship, holography is radically revolutionizing the spiritual VR landscape.

6.5. The Age of Personalized Immersive Experiences

Arguably, one of the most profound impacts of technological advancements on virtual religions has been the democratization of personalized experiences. Adaptation algorithms, personalized avatars, and AI-based systems allow users to tailor their VR spiritual experiences based on their preferences, needs, and limitations.

The flexibility to personalize the virtual worship experience greatly enhances its emotional resonance, inclusivity, accessibility, and appeal. Whether it's customizing the aesthetics of a virtual sacred space or creating an inclusive environment accommodating the diverse needs of their faith communities, the possibilities are endless and deeply empowering.

In essence, these technological breakthroughs have been instrumental in not merely transforming VR into a powerful tool for religious practice, but also in making the virtual spiritual experience more immersive, intimate, and personalized. As we move forward, these innovations hold the promise of further enriching the spiritual journey in the digital realm, bringing us closer to a future that seamlessly integrates faith and technology.

Chapter 7. The Psychology of Virtual Worship: A Deeper Dive

The quest for understanding the psychology of virtual worship, an intriguing subfield of both psychology and religious studies, is an expedition into the cognitive mechanisms that facilitate religious experiences in digital realms. As we navigate the intricate nexus of the human psyche, technology, and spiritual practices, we unveil revelations about how immersive technologies like virtual reality (VR) are altering both the perception and practice of worship.

7.1. The Connection Between The Mind And Spiritual Experiences

Currently, the intersection between the mind and spirituality is being illuminated by the rising dawn of neurotheology, a discipline that plays an instrumental role in explicating the link between neural activities and spiritual experiences. Positioned at this crossroads, neurotheology seeks to decipher the spiritual resonance in our neural pathways and how technology like VR can stimulate this resonance.

A growing body of research has demonstrated that spiritual experiences could be associated with enhanced activity across various brain regions such as the inferior parietal lobule and the prefrontal cortex, areas related to self-awareness, emotional regulation, and empathy. While VR could directly tap into these brain areas, it also opens up new avenues to leverage the brain's neuroplasticity, which allows the brain to adapt and evolve, aligning robustly with the ever-evolving nature of spiritual practices.

7.2. Virtual Reality: Awakening The Senses

At the heart of the conversation about virtual worship is the concept of embodiment, which is a sense of selfhood that extends to our perceived awareness in a virtual space. VR technologies have mastered the creation of convincing simulations that could elicit the same mental and physiological responses as in real-life scenarios. Practically, this means that VR experiences could awaken our senses, emotions, and cognitions in ways that closely mirror experiences in physical places of worship.

The amplified sensory input mean users could 'feel' the resonance of a chant, 'see' the grandeur of a cathedral, 'touch' sacred symbols, 'smell' fragrant incense all while sitting comfortably at their own homes. This radical shift of sensory perception could fundamentally alter the way worshipers connect to their faith, allowing them to construct an intimate, sensory-rich, and personal relationship with their spiritual practice and beliefs.

7.3. Personalizing The Path To Faith

Addressing the broader topic of personalizing the path to faith, it's important to acknowledge that faith is an intensely personal and variable experience, where different individuals may have distinct ways of connecting to their spiritual reservoir. VR, with its ability to curate customized religious experiences, could offer new pathways to individuals who find traditional forms of worship either inaccessible or less preferable.

Using VR, an individual could orchestrate their personal spiritual journey, choosing and modulating elements that resonate with their understanding of faith, thereby nurturing a more intimate connection with their spiritual self. This paves a new path, offering a personalized and emotive reality, giving users autonomy over their religious experiences, promoting spiritual empowerment.

7.4. The Innovation of Collective Worship in Virtual Spaces

A significant aspect of the psychology of virtual worship revolves around collective experiences of worship. Numerous studies have suggested that collective practices often amplify spiritual resonance, establishing a sense of community and shared beliefs. The advent of VR introduces innovation into conventional methods, enabling remote collective worship in designed virtual spaces, thus bridging geographical limitations.

Groups of people can congregate in virtual places of worship to conduct rituals, celebrations, and discussions, fostering a sense of camaraderie and connectedness. In these digital spaces, prayers can be amplified, silences can be shared, and spiritual support can be extended, building upon the psychological aspects of community bonding, shared experiences, and collective resonance.

7.5. Ethereal Experiences: The Role of Presence in Virtual Worship

A crucial cognitive aspect that VR profoundly influences is the sense of 'presence' – the subjective feeling of being 'inside' the virtual environment, which is amplified through immersive VR experiences. Such feelings of presence can significantly contribute to the emotional depth of the virtual worship experience. It helps individuals psychologically 'transport' into the highly-simulated, realistic virtual environments, thereby facilitating a deeply immersive and emotionally resonant experience akin to real-world religious settings.

Presence can be categorized into two primary facets: personal presence refers to an individual's psychological and physiological engagement with the VR experience, while social presence pertains to the perceived intimacy and immediacy of interactions with other individuals or entities within the VR space. Both forms of presence play significant roles in immersive virtual worship, offering a sense of authenticity akin to physical religious practices and ceremonies.

In conclusion, the psychology of virtual worship is a deep and captivating subject that invites curiosity, study, and exploration. The interplay between immersive technologies like VR and the human psyche lays the groundwork for fresh perspectives on the practice and experience of worship, forging new bonds between age-old spirituality and contemporary technology. By engaging the senses, personalizing faith experiences, facilitating collective worship in virtual spaces, and cultivating a heightened sense of presence, VR is poised to reshape our relationship with spirituality in the digital age.

Chapter 8. Potential Challenges and Ethical Considerations of VR in Religion

Amid the remarkable advancements ushering a new era of immersive and interactive religious and spiritual experiences, there also reside potential challenges intertwined with the use of virtual reality (VR) technology in religious practices. These issues do not simply reflect in terms of technical hazards or setbacks, but signify deeper ethical inquiries and concerns that necessitate thoughtful deliberation as we progress further into the digital future of faith practices.

8.1. The Digital Divide: Access and Equity

A key obstacle to the integration of virtual reality in religious practices is perhaps the accessibility and affordability of VR technology. While VR holds immense promise, it is largely available to those who can afford the equipment and have access to high-speed internet. This creates a digital divide, where a significant proportion of the global population might not have opportunities to engage in virtual spiritual practices. It thus becomes essential to consider how technology can be made more inclusive, ensuring it doesn't inadvertently create a religious divide or exacerbate existing socioeconomic disparities.

8.2. The Question of Authenticity and Sacred Spaces

As VR technology seeks to replicate and replace physical sacred spaces, the question of authenticity inevitably surfaces. Religious experiences are often deeply tied to specific sacred sites, with their associated histories, traditions, and community connections. Digitizing these experiences might lead to reductionist views, where nuanced spiritual dynamics could potentially be lost. A comprehensive discussion on maintaining the sanctity and authenticity of these spaces in virtual environments, while promoting the added convenience and accessibility, is therefore paramount.

8.3. The Possibility of Misrepresentation

Given the power of VR to create alternate realities, there lies the risk of misrepresentation or misinterpretation of religious elements. The potential for misuse is significant, particularly if the technology falls into hands that do not understand or respect the complexities of religious iconography, ritual, or narrative. This accentuates the need for careful curation of content by religious and cultural experts, ensuring accurate depiction of religious practices.

8.4. The Experiences of Vulnerable Groups

With the advent of VR, special attention must be given to the experiences of vulnerable populations, such as the disabled, elderly, or those dealing with emotional or mental health issues. It's imperative to consider how they would interact with virtual religious environments, and how the technology could be made more user-friendly and supportive for them. Behavioral health experts and technologists can collaborate to design VR environments tailored to each user's unique needs and abilities, creating truly inclusive virtual spaces.

8.5. Data Privacy and Security Concerns

In an age marked by continuous debates over data privacy, concerns regarding rights and protection in virtual religious environments are equally pressing. Users' data could be subjected to misuse, or unauthorized intrusion by malicious entities. As such, robust security measures and stringent data handling norms must be implemented to ensure the safety and privacy of users.

8.6. The Potential for Spiritual Consumerism

While the digitalization of religious practices may make them more accessible, there is growing concern that it also risks reducing spiritual experiences and practices to a form of consumerism. The notion of "virtual reality faith" commodified and commercialized is not only an ethical concern, but also a theological one. This aspect necessitates serious reflection and debate among stakeholders to endorse a balanced approach, harmoniously merging the accessibility of technology and the sanctity of spiritual practices.

8.7. Building Ethical Guidelines

Lastly, instituting ethical guidelines for the development and use of VR in religious practices is critical to prevent misuse and ensure respectful representation. These guidelines can help technologists and religious practitioners maintain a fine balance - innovating while preserving sacred traditions, respecting diversity and individual faith choices.

In summary, the intersection of virtual reality and religion introduces myriad ethical and practical challenges that necessitate serious debate and thoughtful regulation. With collaborative, interdisciplinary approaches, we can navigate these challenges to realize the full potential of virtual spaces in fostering enriched, inclusive, and enlightened spiritual practices. Moreover, maintaining a firm ethical grounding as we innovate, ensures that we advance technologically without compromising the very essence of the spiritual experiences we seek to enhance. The journey is complex, yet the potential gains - in terms of accessibility, inclusivity, and personalized spiritual journeys - are worth the endeavor. This exploration, however, calls for responsibility, vigilance, and respect towards the sanctity of religious practices within the digital realm. The ethical and moral compass guiding us in our physical interactions will need to extend, perhaps with even greater force, within these unfolding virtual landscapes of faith.

Chapter 9. The Future of VR in Faith Practices: Expert Predictions

Technologies like Virtual Reality (VR) are acting as disruptive forces, metamorphosing not just commercial industries but also less conventional fields like spirituality and religion. As we stand on the precipice of the future, we shall delve into the transformative potential that VR holds for faith practices, drawing upon the manifold insights offered by seasoned experts, scholars, technologists, and religious leaders.

9.1. Anticipating the Technological Evolution

In contemplating the future of VR in religious practices, it's essential to first examine the evolution of technology. VR, in its current state, primarily uses headsets to provide a three-dimensional simulation of a real or imagined environment. The technology is steadily maturing, with key improvements in sound, haptic feedback, and visual quality. Looking forward, experts predict even more immersive and intricate experiences.

These future VR systems are expected to be more seamless and intuitive, stimulating not just sight and sound but potentially smell, taste, and even emotions. As one expert commented, "VR might eventually allow us to simulate a digital twin of our reality, forming a more profound religious experience than ever before."

9.2. Addressing Inclusivity and Accessibility

Inclusivity and accessibility have been constant topics of discussion with VR's current applications, extending into its future within religion as well. Many experts view VR as a way to bridge the gap between physical constraints and spiritual needs.

The digital future of faith might involve virtual religious communal spaces open to all, irrespective of their physical limitations or geographical restrictions, making religious experiences truly universal. This could potentially lead to virtual religious tourism or pilgrimages, bringing distant sacred sites within reach of anyone with a VR headset.

9.3. The Blend of Ancient Traditions and New Tech

A significant trend noticed during these conversations was the blending of ancient traditions and rituals with the cutting-edge technology. Many theologians and religious leaders believe that VR has the potential to rejuvenate traditional faith practices, make them interactive, and reach younger cohorts without diluting the essence of faith. Driven by realistic virtual reproductions of sacred scriptures, ceremonies, and sites, VR could alter how we engage with religious history, bringing the ancient to the present in an immersive manner.

9.4. Personalization of Spiritual Practices

The concept of personalization is central to many consumer technologies, and experts predict the same for the future of VR in faith practices. Customized religious experiences, such as meditations or prayers tailored to individual needs and preferences, could become commonplace. Personal digital spiritual guides could take the form of AI-powered agents, familiarizing users with different aspects of their faith, answering queries, and promoting deeper understanding and connection.

9.5. The Ethical Landscape

The utilization of VR in faith practices isn't without its dilemmas. Experts caution that appropriate ethical frameworks need to be established to ensure the respectful and sensitive portrayal of religious content. The commodification of sacred spaces and rituals, digital evangelism, and tech addiction are among the many concerns that require careful thought and consideration.

9.6. Future Research and Studies

The future of VR in faith practices promises a wealth of research opportunities. Interdisciplinary studies involving technology, psychology, sociology, and theology could provide valuable insights into the impact of VR on belief systems, community formation, and individual spirituality. Ongoing and future research could shape how we understand and implement technology within a religious context.

At the intersection of faith and technology, VR promises a future where spiritual experiences are not only immersive but accessible, personalized, and continuously evolving. However, the journey towards this future will undoubtedly require sensitivity in preserving religious integrity, balancing tech-hype with genuine spiritual value, and ensuring ethical conduct in this brave new digital world of faith. Experts remain optimistic yet cautious, acknowledging that while VR could revolutionize faith experiences, it is not a panacea for all spiritual challenges. Instead, it should be seen as a tool for enhancing individual spirituality and community bonds, while respecting the sanctity of age-old traditions. Thus ends our profound exploration into the future of VR in faith practices.

Chapter 10. Next Generation Faith- VR Impact on Younger Cohorts

In an era defined by the surge of digital advances and uncapped technological potential, the lives of young individuals are becoming progressively integrated with technology. Virtual reality (VR) is rapidly weaving its way into the fabric of multiple disciplines, including education, entertainment, health, and now, religion and spiritual experiences. When we consider the congregation of the future, it bears notice that the younger cohorts are the ones that will shape this new vista of faith, one that is increasingly digitized and virtually rendered.

10.1. The Digital Natives: Boundlessly Tech-Savvy

It is critical to recognize that the current generation of youngsters are digital natives, having been raised in an environment imbued with technology, they are at ease with embracing and employing novel technological advancements with little to no trepidation. This unique trait makes them optimally positioned to integrate VR into their religious and spiritual practices. Whether it is participating in a VR rendition of a religious pilgrimage, a virtually led prayer or meditation session, or an immersive educational program detailing the chronicles of their faith, VR affords this younger generation the resources to experience their spirituality in a vastly more personalized, digitally enriched, and immersive manner.

10.2. VR: The New Medium for Faith Formation

Virtual reality is being increasingly considered as the next frontier for faith formation among the younger cohorts. It can serve as a technologically sophisticated conduit to impart religious knowledge, morals, values, and spiritual wellness. VR technology's ability to simulate distant places, pivotal historical times, or advanced philosophical concepts provides an interactive tool that can engage the young in the narratives central to their religious heritage. In comparison to the static, text-centered ways of traditional religious study, the realistic, participatory nature of VR might appeal to younger individuals, manifesting in increased interest and engagement in religious teachings and practices.

10.3. Virtual Worship: A Sophisticated Blend of Tradition and Innovation

VR can redefine how the youth engage with worship. For instance, congregations can convene in a virtual place of worship, allowing for group experiences that transcend geographical boundaries. This ability could cater significantly to the younger cohorts, who value connectivity and inclusion and often move across cities or countries for education or work. VR's potential for creating deeply immersive experiences might also resonate positively with the contemporary yearning among younger people for personalized, meaningful religious interactions.

10.4. Opportunities for Broader Spiritual Exploration

Furthermore, the application of VR in faith and spirituality proffers opportunities for the youth to explore a wider array of spiritual practices; it functions as a portal that not only makes accessible their own traditions but also other faiths and spiritual movements. The significance of this potential lays in its ability to enhance religious tolerance - a value often championed by the tech-savvy, progressive younger generations.

10.5. Ethical Considerations Specific to Younger Cohorts

While VR portends monumental shifts in how the younger cohorts navigate their spiritually, attempting to forecast its total impact would be premature. Certain questions persist-particularly associated with the interplay between personal data, privacy, ethical concerns around VR content creation, and its potentially addictive nature. As we acknowledge the change VR brings, it is essential to also carefully consider how these changes intersect with the lives of the target demographic and strive to curate experiences that are not just engaging, but ethically founded and thoughtfully constructed as well.

10.6. Forward-Looking Perspective: The Future of Faith

In conclusion, while the integration of VR in religion bears many promises, navigating its use wisely necessitates a deep understanding of the unique needs, interests, and constraints of the younger cohorts. The myriad ways VR could influence faith practices may dramatically shift the status quo, necessitating proactive discussion, guidance, and leadership from those at the helm of religious institutions on how to best serve their youngest members in this new digital age of faith. The next generation's faith, hence, could very possibly be defined by the intersectionality of spirituality and advanced technology, blurring lines between the tangible and the virtual, the traditional and the innovative. It is a new world, resplendent in opportunities, and the journey towards understanding it has just begun.

Chapter 11. Cultivating Your Own Virtual Spirituality: A Practical Guide

In the rapidly evolving landscape of technology-driven faith practices, cultivating one's own virtual spirituality emerges as an exercise intertwining the eternal tenets of faith with the infinite possibilities of virtual reality (VR). Virtual spirituality, given its inherently personalized nature, presents a unique opportunity for individuals to explore, experience, and embody their faith in ways that resonate with their personal beliefs, spiritual inclinations, and technological comforts. This in-depth, meticulous, and exhaustive exploration aims to guide you through this process of nurturing your virtual spirituality, and sets out practical steps to make your transition into this new realm as smooth and enlightening as possible.

11.1. Understanding Your Spiritual Needs

A comprehensive understanding of your spiritual needs is the preliminary, yet critical step that is instrumental in shaping your virtual religious experience. The vastness of VR in religion caters to a spectrum of believers – from the devoutly traditional to the innovatively contemporary. An initial assessment of aspects such as your religious beliefs and orientation, the importance of community unity versus personal solitude in prayer, and the degree of technological interplay you are comfortable with, will help you identify the ideal range within the VR faith spectrum that will be conducive to your spiritual growth. Engaging in introspective exercises or discussions with faith leaders could be fruitful in discerning these substantive elements.

11.2. Selecting an Appropriate VR Platform

The next step entails choosing a VR platform that caters to your religious needs and aligns seamlessly with your spiritual objectives. Numerous leading tech corporations and independent start-ups offer a variety of VR applications that replicate traditional places of worship, hold virtual religious gatherings, facilitate immersive pilgrimage experiences, and provide interactive Scripture study. Evaluating factors such as the realism of the virtual environment, the technological and financial accessibility, the spectrum of religious content available, and the degree of interactivity, will assist you in identifying a platform most suited to your spiritual aspirations.

11.3. Augmenting Your Virtual Worship Experience

Once you have adapted to the chosen VR platform, the next phase involves enriching your virtual worship experience. You can do so by incorporating elements that enhance the spiritual ambience, integrating consistent spiritual rituals, and personalising the virtual surroundings to align with your unique spiritual inclinations. For instance, you can decorate your virtual space with significant religious symbols, or incorporate ethereal hymns that create the desired mood. Regularly partaking in VR religious ceremonies or meditation sessions could also bolster your spiritual growth.

11.4. Navigating the Challenges of VR Spirituality

Despite the expansive opportunities offered by VR, it is vital to be cognizant of the potential difficulties you may encounter in your virtual spirituality pursuit. An overreliance on VR could detract from the essence of physical religious practices and communal bonding in real-world congregations. It is thereby essential to achieve a balanced amalgamation of traditional and VR-based faith practices. Handling technological hiccups such as connectivity issues, VR-induced motion sickness, or hardware malfunctions, requires patience and a basic troubleshooting knowledge.

11.5. Maintaining Ethical and Safe Conduct in Virtual Spaces

In the realm of virtual spirituality, it is critical to adhere to ethical guidelines and safe conduct. This entails respecting the virtual spaces of others, refraining from hateful or derogatory comments, and maintaining the sanctity of the virtual place of worship. You should also take steps to protect your digital privacy, such as using secure connections, protecting personal identification information, and being aware of the data collection and privacy policies of your chosen VR platform.

11.6. Embracing the Future: The Next Steps in Your Virtual Spiritual Journey

As you transcend the initial steps of your journey and transition into a regular virtual worshipper, it is worth exploring next-gen VR technologies that may deepen your spiritual experience. Investing in higher-quality VR hardware, participating in global virtual spiritual events, or even collaborating with VR developers to create personalized religious content could prove immensely invigorating to your spiritual voyage.

In sum, the cultivation of personal virtual spirituality involves a nuanced understanding of one's spiritual needs, an informed selection of a compatible VR platform, a continual enrichment of the virtual faith experience, alongside navigation of potential challenges and maintenance of ethical conduct. As we make strides into the future, the burgeoning opportunities in VR religion foretell an exciting horizon for those seeking to traverse the spiritual landscape of the digital age. Embrace this journey with an open mind and a resilient spirit, and you may find yourself entering a new epoch of spirituality, one that beautifully marries tradition with innovation, bringing the sacred even closer to the realm of the everyday.

Immerse, explore, and experience – your spiritual awakening in the virtual space awaits.

www.ingramcontent.com/pod-product-compliance
Lightning Source LLC
La Vergne TN
LVHW051627050326
832903LV00033B/4697